DISCOVER...

THE ANCIENT EGYPTIANS

Illustrated by
Isabel Greenberg

Written by
Imogen Greenberg

Frances Lincoln
Children's Books

Welcome To Ancient Egypt

Ancient Egyptian civilisation lasted for thousands of years, ruled over by the great pharaohs. Everyone has heard of the famous Pharaoh TutanKhamun. But who were the Egyptians really?

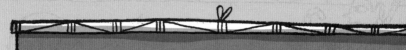

The Egyptian pharaohs united Egypt as one Kingdom and ruled all the way down the great river Nile. They ruled for thousands of years, and built huge pyramids in the desert. They became rich because of the fertile land around the Nile. Though they fought their neighbours, they were rarely conquered, because Egypt was so well protected by rivers and deserts.

The Egyptians invented and discovered many things in art, engineering and science, and the GreeKs and Romans borrowed all sorts of clever ideas from them. You might recognise some of them! Did you Know the Egyptians invented the first calendar in the world with 365 days, just like the one we use?

Today, we Know a lot about the Egyptians, thanKs to archaeologists and historians. Archaeologists have discovered artefacts, temples and pyramids covered in Egyptian hieroglyphics. Historians cracked the code of hieroglyphics, so we can read all about the Egyptians in their own words.

In this book, you will discover all sorts of secrets about the Egyptians... And if you're wondering where and when all these things happened, turn to the back, where you will find a FOLD-OUT MAP and TIMELINE OF EVENTS. Now there's nothing left to do except meet your guide!

PHARAOHS

PHARAOHS ruled Ancient Egypt and were the head of the government and the high priest of every temple. The Egyptians believed the Gods watched over the pharaohs as they ruled.

THE OLD KINGDOM
2686 — 2181 BC

Djoser was the first pharaoh of the Old Kingdom and he ruled Egypt from the capital at MEMPHIS. He was the first pharaoh to be buried in a pyramid.

THE MIDDLE KINGDOM, 2055 — 1650 BC

In the Middle Kingdom, the capital moved to THEBES. While the first pharaohs were buried in huge pyramids, these pharaohs were buried in hidden tombs underground, nearly impossible to find.

THE NEW KINGDOM, 1150 — 1069 BC

These pharaohs expanded the borders of Egypt, waging war against other lands. They were buried in the VALLEY OF THE KINGS, in tombs filled with treasure and gold.

1. PHARAOH

Ancient Egyptian society was structured in a strict hierarchical system, with the richest and most powerful at the top, and the poorest at the bottom. At the very top was the pharaoh, who ruled over everyone and everything.

3. NOBLES AND PRIESTS

Nobles were powerful families who ruled regions of Egypt on behalf of the pharaoh, making laws and keeping order. Priests performed ceremonies to the god of their temple, and made sure that the gods were happy.

And happy gods mean a happy Egypt!

Corn: lots
Grain: lots
Cattle: lots...

5. SOLDIERS

Soldiers were important, and many noble families sent their second sons to the army (they couldn't risk the heir). Soldiers were rewarded for their hard work with gifts of land.

Ya!

7. FARMERS AND SLAVES

Farmers rented land from the rich nobles and pharaohs, farming it in return for a house. Slaves were at the bottom of society, and were often prisoners captured in war. They worked on farms, in mines and quarries, and sometimes in temples.

2589 – 2566 BC
KHUFU was the most important pharaoh of the Old Kingdom. He built the Great Pyramid of Giza as his tomb, and he was buried there after he died.

2570 – 2544 BC
KHAFRE was the son of Khufu. He built the second largest pyramid at Giza, to sit next to his father's.

1473 – 1458 BC
HATSHEPSUT was a pharaoh of the New Kingdom. She was unusual because she was a female pharaoh. She built a huge and beautiful temple near Luxor named after her.

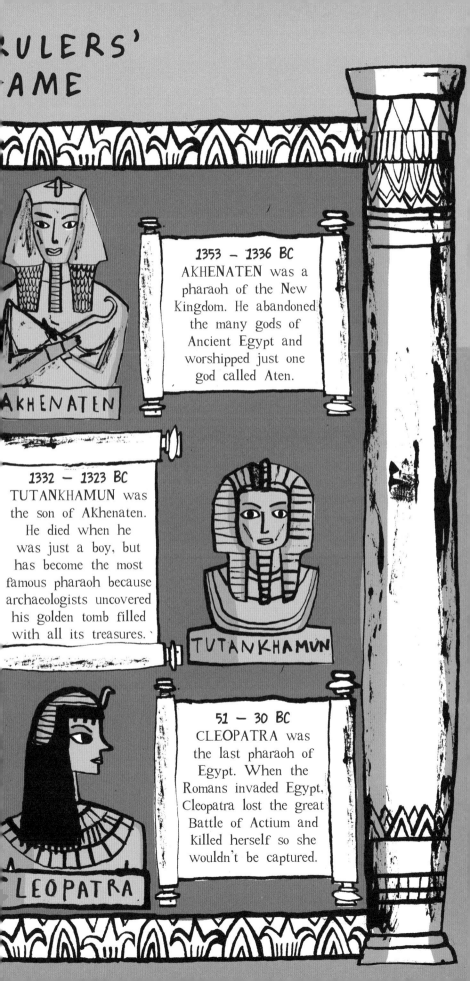

1353 – 1336 BC
AKHENATEN was a pharaoh of the New Kingdom. He abandoned the many gods of Ancient Egypt and worshipped just one god called Aten.

AKHENATEN

1332 – 1323 BC
TUTANKHAMUN was the son of Akhenaten. He died when he was just a boy, but has become the most famous pharaoh because archaeologists uncovered his golden tomb filled with all its treasures.

TUTANKHAMUN

51 – 30 BC
CLEOPATRA was the last pharaoh of Egypt. When the Romans invaded Egypt, Cleopatra lost the great Battle of Actium and killed herself so she wouldn't be captured.

CLEOPATRA

Ramesses II was a ferocious fighter, and went on many campaigns. He fought the NUBIANS, to the south of Egypt. He also went on many campaigns into Asia and Syria against the HITTITES and their allies. He marched into battle with his sons.

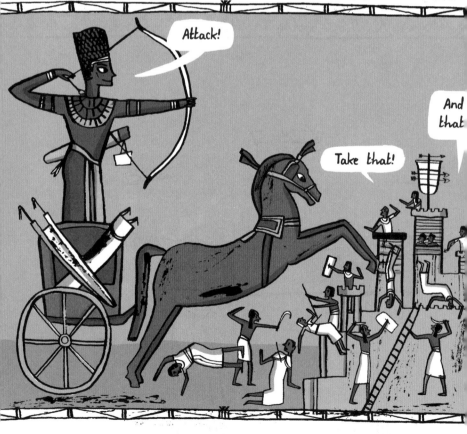

After many years, Ramesses signed a peace treaty with the Hittites.

Ramesses II had many wives, and hundreds of children. Some historians estimate he had over 100 sons and over 50 daughters!

Of all his wives, the principal queen was NEFERTARI, mother of the oldest prince, his heir.

Ramesses' huge temple, ABU SIMBEL, took 20 years to build. It was cut into a rock face, with colossal statues of himself at the front. It was positioned so that the sun's rays pointed straight inside on two days of the year: his birthday and coronation day (historians think).

His tomb is in the VALLEY OF THE KINGS, and takes up more space than any other pharaoh's. Although his tomb is very impressive, the tomb of his wife Nefertari in the Valley of the Queens is even more famous. It is covered in beautiful paintings, all of Nefertari...

... and not a single one of my husband!

EGYPTIAN RELIGION

The Egyptians worshipped many gods. The first pharaohs said their power came from the god Ra and called themselves 'The Son of Ra'.

RA was the GOD OF THE SUN. He was a human with the head of a falcon, crowned by a sun disc and a sacred cobra. The Ancient Egyptians believed Ra created the world and was the most important god of all.

Each day, I, Ra, sail to the heavens in a boat. At night, I sail into the underworld to do battle with Chaos, and leave the moon to light the night sky.

There was a calendar of popular RELIGIOUS FESTIVALS. Everyone joined in and they were a time of indulgence. Ordinary people weren't allowed inside temples, so festivals were an important time for them to worship the gods.

Hold it steady there, boys...

After a while the pharaohs began to worship another god, AMUN, which means 'hidden one'.

I'm Amun. First, I created myself, and then I created everything else!

Then the pharaohs started to worship both gods together, and called him AMUN-RA. He could appear as a man or a ram.

In the New Kingdom, OPET was the most important festival. It was celebrated at Karnak and lasted for three weeks. The priests processed the statues of the god Amen, taking them on a short journey down the Nile before they returned to the temple.

We had other celebrations too, like the coronation day of a new pharaoh.

THE STORY OF ISIS AND OSIRIS

Seth brutally MURDERED his brother Osiris. Isis found his body and brought him back to life, long enough for them to have a son, Horus. Then Osiris became the god of the underworld. His death and resurrection were symbolic of the death and regrowth of crops.

The gods let Horus decide what happened to Seth...

And Horus BANISHED him to the desert for murdering his father.

But after Seth was banished, he still protected the SUN BARGE of the god Ra each night, as he journeyed through the underworld.

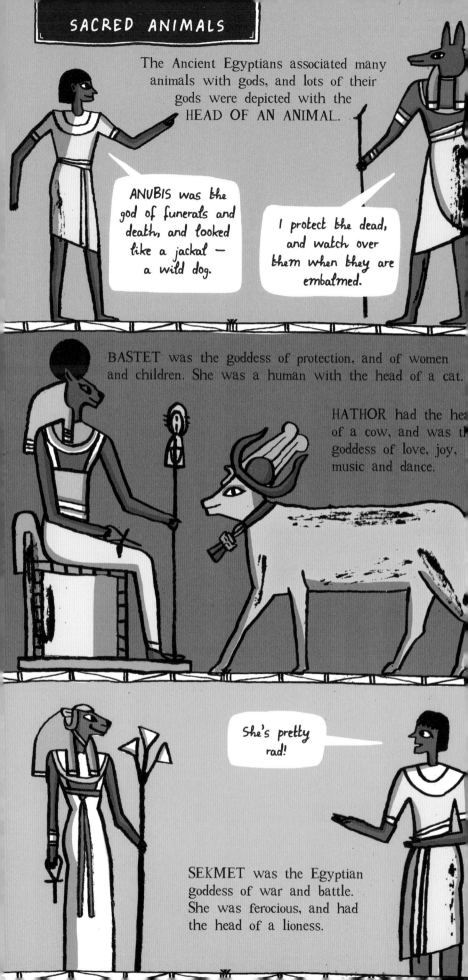

SACRED ANIMALS

The Ancient Egyptians associated many animals with gods, and lots of their gods were depicted with the HEAD OF AN ANIMAL.

ANUBIS was the god of funerals and death, and looked like a jackal — a wild dog.

I protect the dead, and watch over them when they are embalmed.

BASTET was the goddess of protection, and of women and children. She was a human with the head of a cat.

HATHOR had the head of a cow, and was the goddess of love, joy, music and dance.

She's pretty rad!

SEKMET was the Egyptian goddess of war and battle. She was ferocious, and had the head of a lioness.

CATS IN ANCIENT EGYPT

The most sacred animal in Ancient Egypt was the CAT. The Egyptians farmed all of the fertile land of Egypt, and mice, rats and snakes would damage crops. The wild cats of Egypt helped keep these animals away, and some Egyptians even trained cats to hunt with them.

There were very high penalties for harming a cat in Egypt. At some points in Egyptian history, it even carried the death penalty.

When a cat died, their owners would go in to deep mourning and shave their eyebrows! The cat was then MUMMIFIED and buried with provisions like milk, mice and rats.

Crocodiles, hawks and cows were associated with the gods. Scarab beetles were also sacred animals.

The Egyptians also mummified these animals. One crocodile mummy was found buried with 40 babies, all wrapped in linen, on its back.

CLEVER EGYPTIANS!

The ancient Egyptians, especially the scribes and the priests, dedicated a lot of time to learning.

That's Venus.

I bet you say that to all the girls.

STARGAZING

The ASTRONOMERS of Ancient Egypt knew about five of the planets, and cleverly observed that Mercury and Venus moved around the sun. After centuries of studying the sky, some Egyptians even worked out that the Earth was a globe, and guessed how big it was all the way round.

CALENDARS

The ancient Egyptians built a CALENDAR OF THE YEAR, which had 365 days in it. Astronomers could predict the day on which the Nile flooding would begin with their calendar. When the flood was on its way, the star Sirius rose in the sky.

Get ready lads, the floods are coming!

ENGINEERING

The TEMPLES and the PYRAMIDS were orientated with great precision. Temples pointed to the horizon at the place where the sun would appear on the morning of the summer solstice.

LIBRARIES

The ancient Egyptians gathered all their writing and learning in libraries. When the Romans invaded, the GREAT LIBRARY OF ALEXANDRIA was supposed to be the biggest and most important in the world!

EGYPTIAN CULTURE

The ancient Egyptians wrote in HIEROGLYPHS, a series of symbols that they used instead of an alphabet. Each hieroglyph represented a sound, a letter or an entire word. They could be written in any direction — up or down, right to left or left to right.

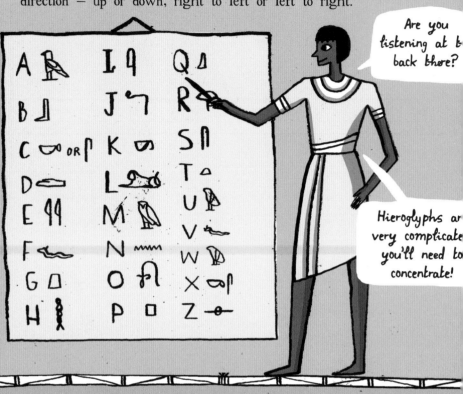

THE ROSETTA STONE

For thousands of years, hieroglyphs were a mystery to historians and archaeologists, and they couldn't understand what they meant. Then they discovered the Rosetta Stone. It has the same text on it in HIEROGLYPHS and in ANCIENT GREEK.

Because they were able to read Ancient Greek, they could unlock the mysteries of Ancient Egyptian hieroglyphs!

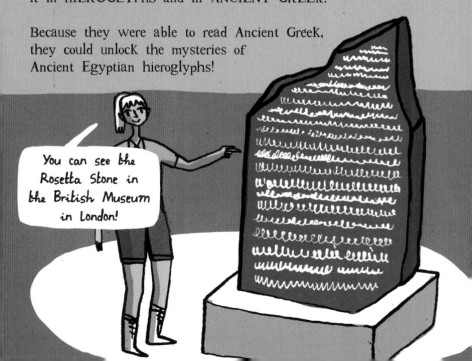

The ancient Egyptians wrote on PAPYRUS. Because of the hot, dry desert sand, some of this papyrus has survived thousands of years.

Hieroglyphics were complicated, and it took many years of training to be a SCRIBE. They started when they were still children.

THE NILE

Ancient Egypt was divided into UPPER and LOWER EGYPT, with the River Nile running through both parts. It's a bit confusing because Upper Egypt was in the south, and Lower Egypt was in the north.

This is because the River Nile flows upwards, from south to north.

The Nile is the longest river in the world...

Ancient Egyptian life revolved around the river Nile because most of Egypt is desert...

... apart from the banks of the river Nile, where the land is fertile because of all the water.

Each year in September, the Nile flooded and provided the land with fresh nutrients so the crops could grow tall. They called the soil from the floods the 'GIFT FROM THE NILE'.

The Egyptians farmed GRAIN, to make bread from, and grew so much that they sold it to other countries and became rich. They also grew flax for their clothes and papyrus for their paper.

The Egyptian seasons were not like ours — they only had three seasons, and they revolved around the river Nile.

AKHET was the first season. It means inundation, and this was the flooding of the Nile.

SHEMU was the harvest season, when we picked all the crops before the flood came.

PERET was the growing season, when the fertile land from the flood helped our crops grow tall.

... It's over 4,000 miles long!

There is an old Egyptian story that the Nile floods came from the tears of the goddess Isis as she cried for her dead husband Osiris.

Most Ancient Egyptian clothing was made from linen, a very light fabric made from the FLAX they harvested from the river banks. It was soaked in water until soft and separated into fibres, which were then spun into thread and woven into cloth.

MEN wore a wraparound skirt that they tied at the waist with a belt. The length depended on what was fashionable at the time.

The more expensive and fine the linen, the more see-through it was. You might have been able to see right through to the pants of rich Egyptian men! Some men also wore jewellery and headdresses.

WOMEN wore full-length dresses with shoulder straps. Like rich men, rich women wore lots of jewellery and sometimes a headdress.

Darling. That dress is so Old Kingdom.

I'll have you know, it's the new look!

Egyptian JEWELLERY included rings, earrings, decorated buttons, necklaces, neck collars and pendants. We Know this because archaeologists have dug these up from the ground. Only the very rich could afford gold and precious stones.

Ordinary people made jewellery from pottery beads, which was much cheaper.

The Egyptians believed they travelled to an AFTERLIFE when they died. They prepared their bodies so the gods would help them travel to paradise. Here's how their bodies were MUMMIFIED.

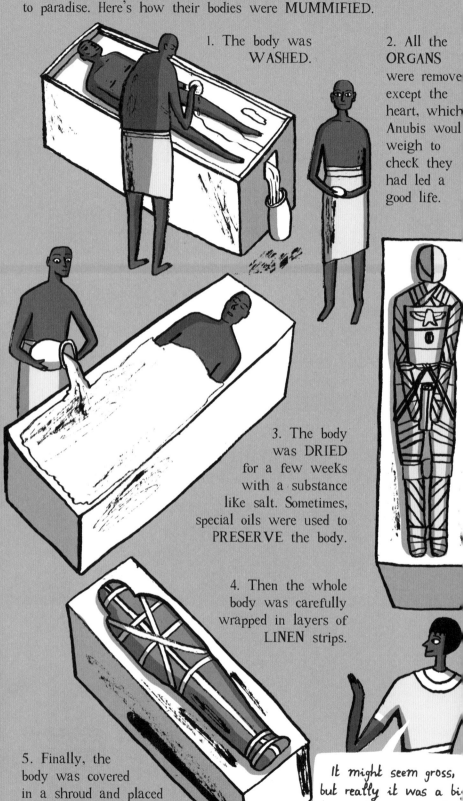

1. The body was WASHED.

2. All the ORGANS were remove except the heart, which Anubis woul weigh to check they had led a good life.

3. The body was DRIED for a few weeks with a substance like salt. Sometimes, special oils were used to PRESERVE the body.

4. Then the whole body was carefully wrapped in layers of LINEN strips.

5. Finally, the body was covered in a shroud and placed inside a coffin called a SARCOPHAGUS.

It might seem gross, but really it was a bi honour for any Egyptia to be mummified!

CANOPIC JARS

Each organ was MUMMIFIED in a special jar, which had the head of a god to protect the organ. The Egyptians didn't think the brain was important, and removed it through the nose and discarded it.

Rich people could have gems and amulets between the layers of linen, and a gold sarcophagus. Some had lots of coffins that fitted inside each other. TUTANKHAMUN had a gold mask of his face.

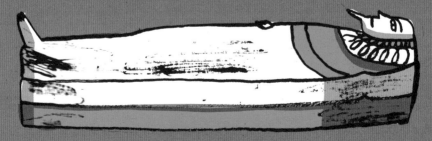

Priests performed ceremonies to make sure the person entered the afterlife. Sometimes spells were painted on their coffin to guide them. Egyptians compiled these spells in the BOOK OF THE DEAD.

PYRAMIDS

The **GREAT PYRAMIDS OF GIZA** are the three biggest pyramids in Egypt and were built by the pharaohs of the Old Kingdom. The Egyptians built their tombs and pyramids on the west bank of the Nile, because that was where the sun set each day, and was associated with the dead and the afterlife.

Pyramids are an **ENGINEERING MARVEL**. Huge blocks of stone were cut from a quarry and dragged through the desert to the pyramid site.

They laid out the stones for the first layer. Historians think that for the higher layers, they had to build **RAMPS** from mud bricks, so they could pull the stones up. At the top, the pyramid was finished with a special block made of shining metal.

Blimey this weighs a tonne!

Heave, lads!

The outside of the pyramid was covered in blocks of white **LIMESTONE**, and smoothed down so the pyramid shone white in the desert, and could be seen for miles.

Historians think the biggest pyramid in Egypt, KHUFU'S huge Pyramid of Giza, was made of over 2 million blocks of stone that weighed nearly 6 million tons, and took over 20 years to build.

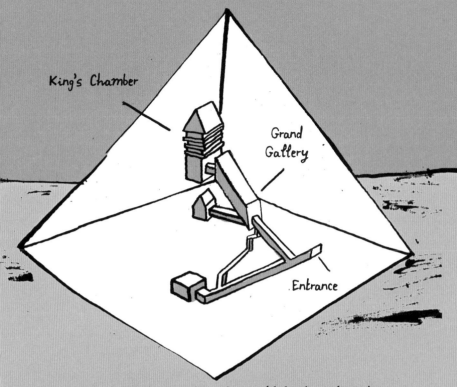

Deep inside the pyramid, the pharaoh would be buried with treasures and items needed to survive in the afterlife. There were twisting TUNNELS and passages that led to the middle. There were trick passages to fool grave robbers but they didn't work, and all the treasures inside are long gone.

The GREAT SPHINX guards the Great Pyramid of Khafre in Giza, and faces the sunrise. A sphinx is a lion with a human head — the head of the pharaoh.

Tombs were often filled with **TREASURES**, because they believed these items were needed for the journey to the afterlife. The richer you were, the more expensive your tomb and treasures were. Because of this, tomb raiders hunted for tombs to steal the treasures. Some were pretty easy to find...

The tombs of important men like pharaohs were sometimes **BOOBY-TRAPPED**, so that tomb raiders couldn't rob them. When the tombs had been robbed, archaeologists found them years later, totally empty...

But some tombs weren't as easy to find and when archaeologists found them, they were untouched!

THE CURSE OF TUTANKHAMUN'S TOMB

The most famous tomb ever discovered was Tutankhamun's. Pharaohs of the New Kingdom were buried in the Valley of the Kings, so archaeologists knew to look there. Lots of the tombs had already been ransacked, but in 1922, HOWARD CARTER and his team found a tomb tucked away behind another one... TUTANKHAMUN'S!

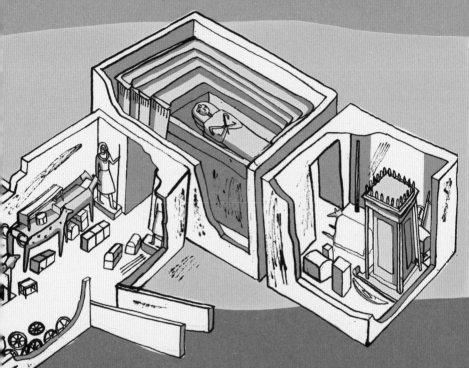

TUTANKHAMUN was a boy king who died suddenly as a teenager and was buried in a hurry, but his tomb was still full of gold, jewels and treasures. (If this was an insignificant pharaoh's tomb, can you imagine what the greatest pharaohs' were like?)

Mysterious things started happening. Things went wrong on site, and members of the team fell ill with strange diseases. Some of them even died. Was this the curse of Tutankhamun?

ISABEL GREENBERG is a London-based comic artist, illustrator and writer. She enjoys illustrating all things historical.

IMOGEN GREENBERG is a London-based writer, who loves to write about history, and is editor of The Story Finders.

Discover... The Ancient Egyptians copyright © Frances Lincoln Ltd 2016
Text copyright © Imogen Greenberg 2016
Illustrations copyright © Isabel Greenberg 2016

The right of Imogen Greenberg to be identified as the author
and Isabel Greenberg to be identified as the illustrator of this work
has been asserted by them in accordance with the Copyright,
Designs and Patents Act, 1988 (United Kingdom).

First published in Great Britain in 2016 by Frances Lincoln Children's Books,
74-77 White Lion Street, London N1 9PF
QuartoKnows.com
Visit our blogs at QuartoKnows.com

A catalogue record for this book is available from the British Library.

ISBN 978-1-84780-825-7
Illustrated digitally
Designed by Nicola Price * Edited by Jenny Broom

Printed in China
1 3 5 7 9 8 6 4 2